FEB 16

D1215451

PATCHWORK ESSENTIALS:

The Half-Square Triangle

JENI BAKER

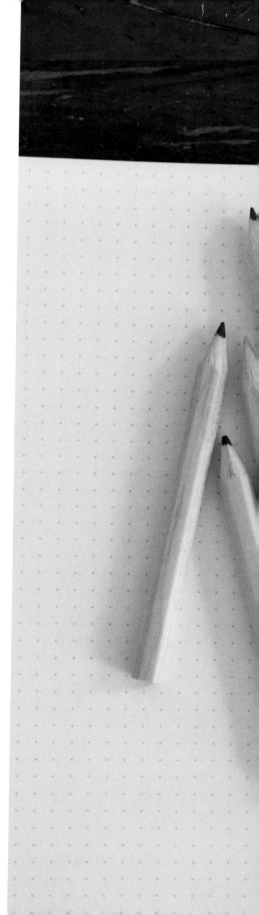

Published in 2015 by Lucky Spool Media, LLC
www.luckyspool.com
info@luckyspool.com

Text ©Jeni Baker
Editor Susanne Woods
Designer Liz Quan
Illustrations Kari Vojtechovsky
Photographer © Lauren Hunt, except inside flaps and
pages 4-11, 14, 18, 19, 23-25, 28, 31-33, 64, 66, and 67
©Jeni Baker and page 128 ©Michael Hanna

Thank you to Amanda Rydell/BE CRAFTY and Laura Hale
for sharing their locations with us for our photoshoots.

All rights reserved. No part of this book may be
reproduced in any form or by any means, electronic, or
mechanical, including photocopying, recording, or by any
information storage and retrieval system without permission in writing from the publisher. Trademarked names (™)
and ® are used throughout the book with no intention of
infringement and to benefit the legal owner. Lucky Spool
Media is a trademark of Lucky Spool Media, LLC.

The information in this book is accurate and complete to
the best of our knowledge. All recommendations are made
without guarantee on the part of the author or Lucky
Spool Media, LLC. The author and publisher disclaim any
liability in connection with this information.

The patterns in this book are copyrighted and must not be
made for resale.

9 8 7 6 5 4 3 2 1

First Edition
Printed in USA

Library of Congress Cataloging-in-Publication
Data available upon request

978-1-940-655-16-1

LSID0028

Acknowledgments

This book was made possible because of some truly awesome people and companies. To Sara at The Sewcial Lounge in Madison, Wisconsin, thank you for your support. I could not ask for a better local shop. To Pat and Walter Bravo at Art Gallery Fabrics, thank you for your guidance and beautiful fabrics to work with. To Melissa of Sew Shabby Quilting, thank you for sharing your talent with me. I would have been hard put to finish all the quilts in this book without you. To Susanne and the Lucky Spool team, thank you for taking a chance on me, and for encouraging me to be myself. Thank you for welcoming me into the Lucky Spool family. It really is an honor to work with you.

Dedication

I would like to dedicate this book to my loving and supportive family, without whom this book would still be a wishful thought. Mom and Dad, thank you for believing in me, and being my biggest fans. I know I sometimes shrug off my accomplishments, but you never do. Michael, your dedication to my happiness and my dreams means so much to me. Thank you for always taking care of me.

The opportunity to write this book would not have happened without my blog readers and the quilters I have met through the online sewing community. To Christina, thank you for encouraging me to start quilting, and for pushing me to write a book. I finally did it! To Jacey and Amanda, thank you for your honest feedback and invaluable friendship. I could not have done this without you.

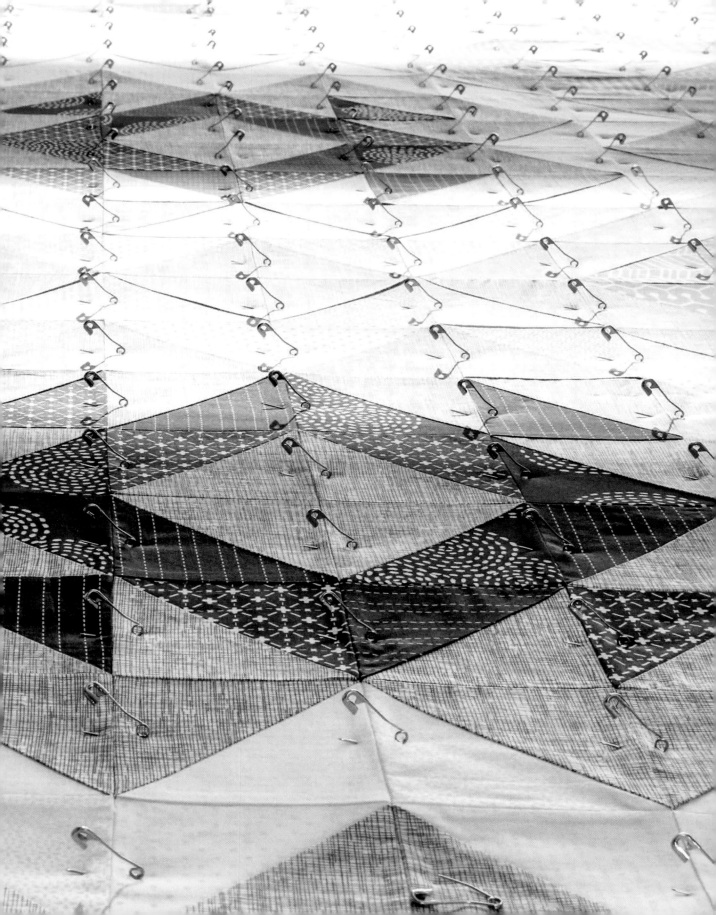

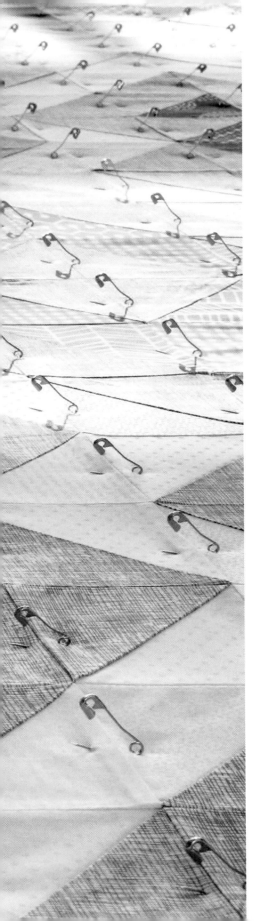

Contents

Introduction

As a child, I was always making things. Whether it was bowls molded from mud in the backyard or collages and friendship bracelets in the craft room, I just wanted to *make*. So it was no surprise that I received a quilting kit when I was around eight years old. I used the kit to make my first "quilt," a pillow for my dolls. It was hand stitched, and rather badly I might add, but I made it.

I did not come back to quilting until 2009, when I was furnishing my first apartment in my junior year of college. I attended a small liberal arts college in northeast Ohio and studied marketing and studio art. I am not exactly sure what sparked the idea, but soon after moving into my apartment, I got the idea to make a patchwork quilt. I had never tackled such a large project, but I dove in headfirst. I consulted the Internet and read as many quilting tutorials as I could find. When it came time to quilt it, I got scared and sent it away to be long arm quilted. I remember tearing open the box when it was returned: it was like Christmas. I immediately bound it and threw it into the wash. I pulled it out of the dryer, all wrinkled and warm. At that moment I knew. I was meant to make quilts.

Quilting is a funny thing. I had no idea how much it would shape my life. It has become my livelihood, and one of the keys to my happiness. I joke that I was destined to be a quilter because I am always cold. It is true, and it is very convenient to have an apartment full of quilts when you live in Wisconsin. As it turns out, quilting also happens to be in my blood. My mom dabbles in quilting, as did many of the women in my family before her. I am the very lucky owner of many of their quilts, and I love knowing that I am doing something that they once did. I quilt for the nostalgia – but, most important, I quilt because it makes me happy.

I have never been one to follow directions when it comes to making something. So it is pretty ironic that I have written a book full of instructions. What I really mean is that I like to learn new things by doing them, and figuring them out for myself. I also happen to like sharing that knowledge with others, which is where the concept of writing this book comes in.

My dad is an entrepreneur, and I learned from an early age that I had the same drive to do things on my own. In college I earned extra money by selling vintage bed sheet fabric and running advertisements on my blog, *In Color Order*. After I graduated and moved to Wisconsin, I had a big decision to make. I could pursue a traditional career path in marketing, or I could figure out a way to make a living in the quilting industry. I chose the harder, more uncertain path, and I am glad that I did. I began writing and publishing my own sewing patterns and, shortly after, designing fabric. In 2011, I began teaching classes locally in Madison, and now here I am, writing a book.

The projects in this book are made up of 2,728 half-square triangles, known as HSTs. If you include the blocks scattered throughout the book and in the block chart, the final count is closer to 4,000. You might be asking yourself, "Is she crazy?". The answer is yes, a little. But honestly, I will make plenty more HSTs in my lifetime. I just love them!

Beyond the twelve quilt patterns in this book, you will also find techniques to assist you in any HST project. I want this to be more than just a pattern book, but a resource for quilters both new and experienced. You will find the tools you need to design your own HST quilts, and the math behind the methods. My true hope is to instill in you a love for these trusty little blocks. Knowledge and practice make all the difference in the world, and I hope through this book you gain a bit of both. Do not be too hard on yourself if your HSTs are not perfect. I can assure you, the quilts and HSTs in this book are not perfect, and that is just fine. So, have fun – and happy HST making!

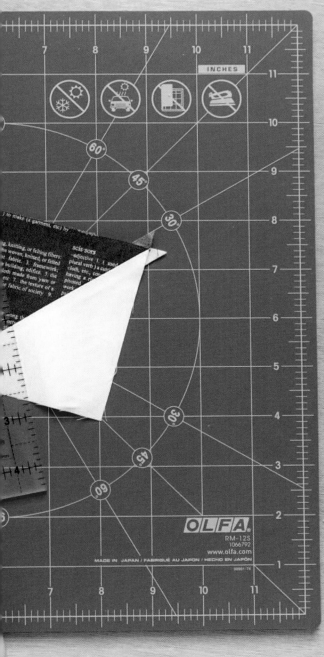

Techniques

Like most things, there is more than one way to sew HSTs. I have chosen to focus on three different methods, but there are many more. There is no perfect method, but there may be one that you prefer over others. Each method has its own benefits, and I encourage you to try each one.

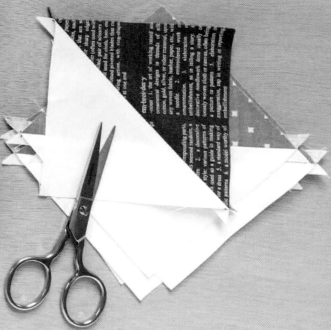

The thing that all of these methods have in common is trimming. Be sure to trim all HSTs according to the individual pattern instructions. I know that trimming down blocks is not the most fun activity, especially when you'd rather just sew.

All I can say is that it is worth it. If you'd like HSTs that are the same size, and accurately finished blocks, trimming is the answer.

TIP Using an accurate ¼" seam allowance is important when doing any kind of quilting, but especially when sewing HSTs. I like to line up the edge of my presser foot with the diagonal line when I sew HSTs. Move your needle until the distance between the edge of the presser foot and the needle is a scant ¼", or use a ¼" presser foot. You may also choose to extend the seam guidelines on your machine bed in order to keep your squares lined up properly. A bit of masking or washi tape works great, and shouldn't leave any sticky residue.

TWO-AT-A-TIME METHOD

I would consider this method the most traditional and widely used method for making HSTs. It is a great place to start if you're new to HSTs. If you're looking for maximum variety in your piecing, this is the best method. This method uses two squares and results in two HSTs.

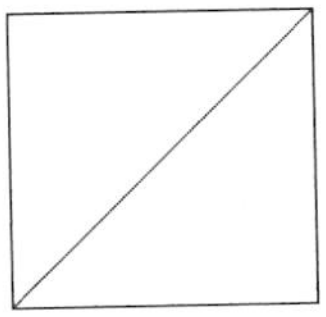

1. On the wrong side of one square, draw a single diagonal line from one corner to another using a marking pen.

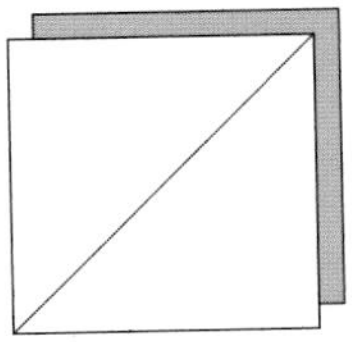

2. Position this and the second square right sides together.

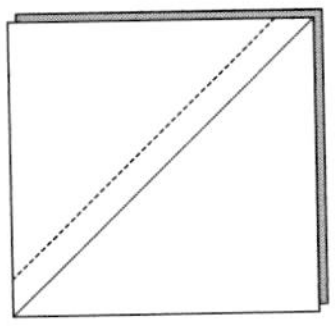

3. Sew ¼" away from one side of the drawn line.

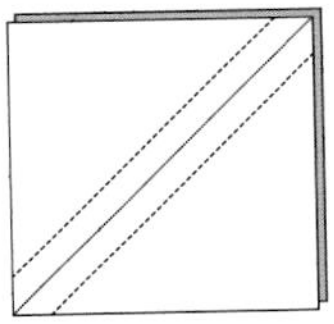

4. Flip the squares around and sew ¼" away from the other side of the drawn line.

5. Cut HSTs apart on the drawn line.

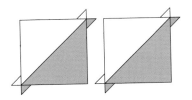

6. Press the seams as desired, then trim.

CREATE ANY SIZE HST

Cut Square Size = Finished HST Size + 1"

EXAMPLE:

Finished HST Size = 6¼"

6¼" + 1"

Cut Square Size = 7¼"

CUT SQUARE SIZE:	TRIM HST TO*:	FINISHED HST SIZE
2"	1½"	1"
2½"	2"	1½"
3"	2½"	2"
3½"	3"	2½"
4"	3½"	3"
4½"	4"	3½"
5"	4½"	4"
5½"	5"	4½"
6"	5½"	5"
6½"	6"	5½"
7"	6½"	6"
7½"	7"	6½"
8"	7½"	7"
8½"	8"	7½"
9"	8½"	8"
9½"	9"	8½"
10"	9½"	9"
10½"	10"	9½"
11"	10½"	10"
11½"	11"	10½"
12"	11½"	11"
12½"	12"	11½"
13"	12½"	12"
13½"	13"	12½"
14"	13½"	13"
14½"	14"	13½"
15"	14½"	14"
15½"	15"	14½"
16"	15½"	15"
16½"	16"	15½"
17"	16½"	16"
17½"	17"	16½"
18"	17½"	17"
18½"	18"	17½"
19"	18½"	18"

*When using a ¼" seam allowance.

FOUR-AT-A-TIME METHOD

This method of making HSTs requires no marking. The resulting HSTs have bias-cut edges, which means they are easily stretched out. I recommend using a starch spray (or alternative) to set the squares before cutting apart the HSTs to help prevent stretching. This method uses two squares and results in four HSTs.

1. Place squares right sides together.

2. Starting in the center of one side, sew ¼" around all four sides, pivoting at each corner. Backstitch to secure stitching. Press square well, using starch spray (or alternative) to set.

  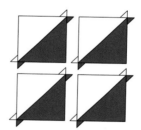

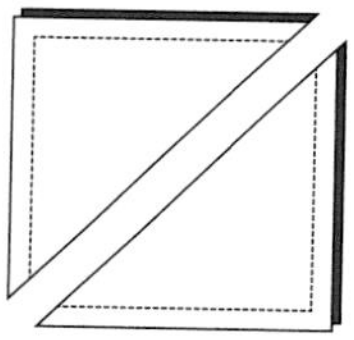

3. Cut square in half along the diagonal, matching corner to corner.

4. Cut in half again along the other diagonal.

5. Press the seams as desired, then trim.

CREATE ANY SIZE HST

The calculation for this method might look intimidating, but just take it one step at a time. Do not forget the order of operations: do things in parenthesis first, then multiplication and division, then addition and subtraction. Round fractions up to the nearest eighth of an inch.

Cut Square Size =
2 x √((Finished HST Size + ¾") ² ÷ 2) + ½"

EXAMPLE:

Finished HST Size: 6¼"

2 x √((6¼" + ¾") ² ÷ 2) + ½"

2 x √((7") ² ÷ 2) + ½"

2 x √(49" ÷ 2) + ½"

2 x √(24½") + ½"

2 x 5" + ½"

10" + ½"

Cut Square Size = 10½"

CUT SQUARE SIZE:	TRIM HST TO*:	FINISHED HST SIZE
3"	1½"	1"
3½"	2"	1½"
4¼"	2½"	2"
5"	3"	2½"
5¾"	3½"	3"
6½"	4"	3½"
7¼"	4½"	4"
8"	5"	4½"
8¾"	5½"	5"
9½"	6"	5½"
10"	6½"	6"
10¾"	7"	6½"
11½"	7½"	7"
12¼"	8"	7½"
13"	8½"	8"
13¾"	9"	8½"
14¼"	9½"	9"
15"	10"	9½"
15¾"	10½"	10"
16½"	11"	10½"
17¼"	11½"	11"
17¾"	12"	11½"
18½"	12½"	12"
19¼"	13"	12½"
20"	13½"	13"
20¾"	14"	13½"
21¼"	14½"	14"
22"	15"	14½"
22¾"	15½"	15"
23½"	16"	15½"
24¼"	16½"	16"
25"	17"	16½"
25½"	17½"	17"
26¼"	18"	17½"
27"	18½"	18"

*When using a ¼" seam allowance.

EIGHT-AT-A-TIME METHOD

This is my personal favorite method for making HSTs. In the other methods, each HST seam is sewn individually. In this method, there are only four seams sewn for eight HSTs, which makes it the most efficient. This method uses two squares and results in eight HSTs.

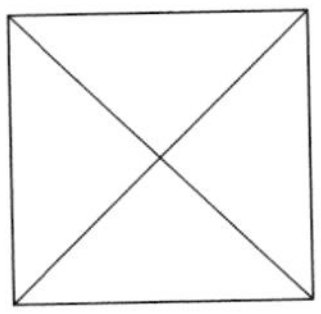

1. On the wrong side of one square, draw two diagonal lines from one corner to another using a marking pen.

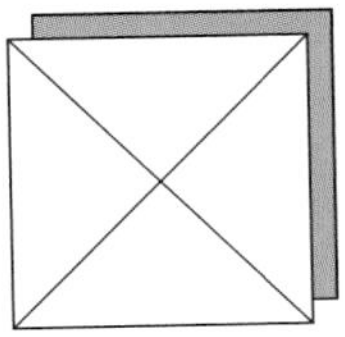

2. Position this and the second square right sides together.

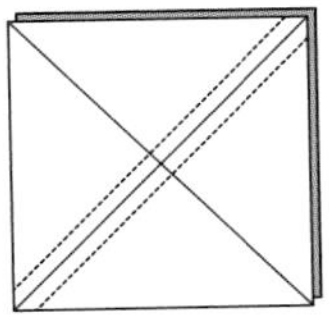

3. Sew ¼" away from the diagonal line on both sides.

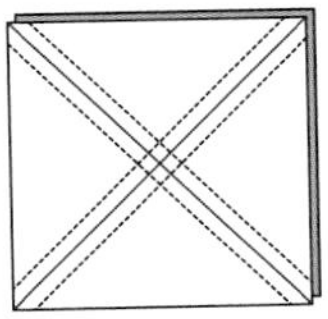

4. Repeat for the remaining diagonal line.

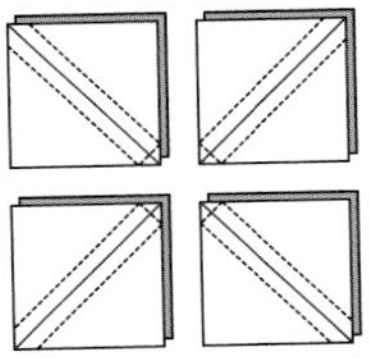

5. Cut square in half. Cut in half again, yeilding four squares.

6. Cut HSTs apart on the drawn lines.

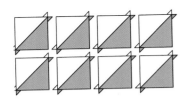

7. Press the seams as desired, then trim.

CREATE ANY SIZE HST

The calculation below is shown as an example.

Cut Square Size =
2 x (Finished HST Size + 1")

EXAMPLE:

Finished HST Size: 6¼"

2 x (6¼" + 1")

2 x 7¼"

Cut Square Size = 14½"

CUT SQUARE SIZE:	TRIM HST TO*:	FINISHED HST SIZE
4"	1½"	1"
5"	2"	1½"
6"	2½"	2"
7"	3"	2½"
8"	3½"	3"
9"	4"	3½"
10"	4½"	4"
11"	5"	4½"
12"	5½"	5"
13"	6"	5½"
14"	6½"	6"
15"	7"	6½"
16"	7½"	7"
17"	8"	7½"
18"	8½"	8"
19"	9"	8½"
20"	9½"	9"
21"	10"	9½"
22"	10½"	10"
22"	11"	10½"
24"	11½"	11"
25"	12"	11½"
26"	12½"	12"
27"	13"	12½"
28"	13½"	13"
29"	14"	13½"
30"	14½"	14"
31"	15"	14½"
32"	15½"	15"
33"	16"	15½"
34"	16½"	16"
35"	17"	16½"
36"	17½"	17"
37"	18"	17½"
38"	18½"	18"

*When using a ¼" seam allowance.

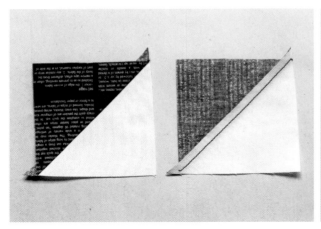

Figure 1

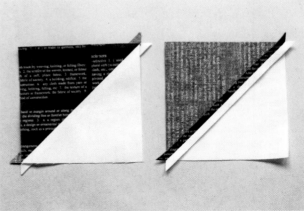

Figure 2

PRESSING

Once your HSTs are sewn, it is important to press them. There is no right or wrong way to press HSTs — the way you choose to press them is up to you. When I am working on a project, I usually have a combination of seams that are pressed open as well as to one side. Either way, do what you feel most comfortable with.

To One Side

Most of the HSTs in this book have their seams pressed to one side. Generally, I press toward the darker fabric or the print fabric **(Fig. 1)**.

Open

The advantage of pressing HST seams open is that it allows them to lay extra flat. This can be especially useful when a project has a lot of intersecting HST seams **(Fig. 2)**.

TRIMMING

The secret to sewing accurate HSTs is in the trimming. All of the HSTs in this book require trimming, and there is excess built into all of the cut square sizes to give you adequate room to trim. Even with careful sewing, it can be difficult to sew perfectly straight lines. Being able to trim down your HSTs **(Fig. 3)** helps make sure they are all the same size and gives you a greater chance of having matching points in your projects.

TIP Rotating cutting mats can help speed up the trimming process. Simply rotate the mat after trimming the first two sides rather than rotating the block itself.

1. After pressing the HST well, lay it right side up on a cutting mat **(Fig. 4)**.

2. Place an acrylic ruler on top of the HST, lining up the diagonal seam with the 45-degree line on the ruler. Position the ruler so that there is excess around the two open sides, as well as excess past the trim size in both directions **(Fig. 5)**.

3. Trim along both edges **(Fig. 6)**.

4. Turn HST 180 degrees and line up the two cut edges with the trim size, aligning the diagonal seam with the 45-degree line on the ruler **(Fig. 7)**.

5. Trim along both edges **(Fig. 8)**.

Figure 3

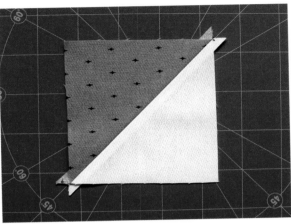

Figure 4

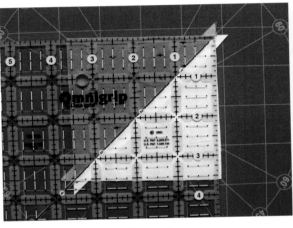

Figure 5

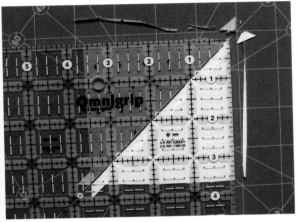

Figure 6

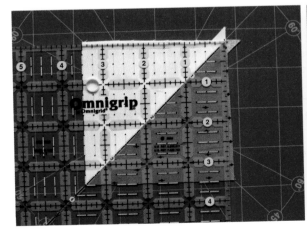

Figure 7

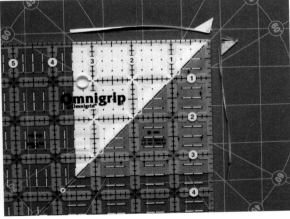

Figure 8

Color Theory

Choosing colors can be paralyzing when starting a new project. I feel perfectly comfortable working with color, but I am still stumped on a regular basis. Having an eye for color comes naturally for some, but it is a learnable skill. I find that it is more an issue of confidence in one's choices. There are some simple color principles that can help you boost your confidence and build foolproof color schemes for your quilts.

The Color Wheel

The basic color wheel shown here in beautiful solids is made up of 12 colors: three primary colors, three secondary colors, and six tertiary colors. The primary colors are red, blue, and yellow. Primary colors are mixed together in different amounts to create all the other colors in the color wheel. The secondary colors are orange, purple, and green. Secondary colors are made up of two primary colors: orange = red + yellow, green = blue + yellow, and purple = blue + red. Tertiary colors are made up of a primary color and a secondary color: red-orange, red-purple, blue-purple, blue-green, yellow-green, and yellow-orange. They are situated between a primary color and a secondary color on the color wheel.

WARM AND COOL COLORS

The color wheel can be split into two halves, warm colors and cool colors. Warm colors are generally considered red-purple through yellow, while cool colors cover yellow-green through purple. Warm colors have a cheerful and happy feeling to them, while cool colors have a more calming and relaxed feeling. When used together, these two color groups provide a lot of contrast. This is explored in Opposites Attract (see page 35).

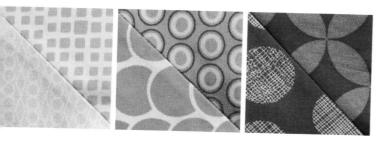

VALUE AND SATURATION

Value is where things start to get complicated in color theory. Different levels of value within a single color are achieved by adding varying amounts of white, gray, and black to that color. In my opinion, this kind of information does not translate very well for the purposes of quilting. Instead, I find it is easier to consider that value describes the lightness or darkness of a color. For example: if red is our base color, dark pink would be a lighter value of red, while pale pink would be a step lighter still.

While value deals with lightness and darkness, saturation deals with how pure a color is. A color with high saturation can be described as vibrant or intense. A color with low saturation can be described as dull or muted. The colors used in Prism (see page 79) all have a similar level of saturation.

NEUTRALS

True neutrals are white, gray, and black. These are achromatic, or without color. They interact well with all the colors on the color wheel, because they do not interfere with the overall color scheme. Quilters often use a lot of cream, beige, and brown as well. These are still considered neutral, but they lean toward the warmer side of the color wheel, so keep that in mind when using them. Neutrals can help calm things down, or add another level of contrast. In Radiant (see page 43), the black and white prints contrast with the strong multi-color scheme. In Convergence (see page 101), neutrals act as the supporting players for a single color.

COLOR SCHEMES

There are many color schemes that can be pulled directly from the color wheel. This is a great place to start when creating a color scheme for a project, or for troubleshooting when a particular color scheme is not working.

Monochromatic

A monochromatic color scheme features a single color. Contrast is created with value or saturation rather than color.

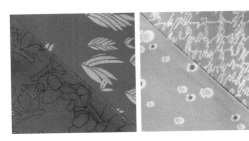

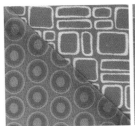

Complementary

Complementary colors are any two colors that are directly across from each other on the color wheel. The contrast between these two colors is at a maximum. Colors that are not directly across from each other still have plenty of contrast, such as the purple and orange shades used in Waypoint (see page 55) and the turquoise and yellow shades used in Getaway (see page 105).

Triadic

Triadic colors are any three colors that are equidistant from one another on the color wheel. This includes our distinct color groups: primary colors, secondary colors, and two groups of tertiary colors. These color schemes are bold and have a lot of contrast. Adjusting the value or saturation can help make these color schemes easier to use, like in Triplicate (see page 75).

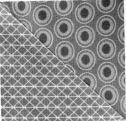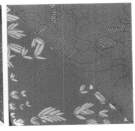

Analogous

Analogous colors are any three or more colors that are right next to one another on the color wheel. These color schemes are much more subtle than other color schemes because there is very little contrast between the colors. To up the excitement, consider adding a color from the opposite side of the color wheel. Many of the quilts in this book use analogous color schemes: Interlocked (see page 39), Woven (see page 61), Citrus Peel (see page 69), and Perspective (see page 109).

COLOR INSPIRATION IS EVERYWHERE

One of my favorite things to do when working on a new fabric collection or quilt design is to go on an inspiration scavenger hunt. Do something with the express purpose of looking for color inspiration. You do not have to go far to discover interesting color schemes and patterns. I like to dig through my closet, collections and craft supplies. When I want to wander a little farther from home, the local antique mall never disappoints.

The Projects

Color Emphasis

CHAPTER 1

Color is a powerful thing, and we each experience color differently.
In this chapter, we will look at how three quilts use color to create a
unique impact, through the emphasis and placement of color. By
exploring contrast through value and pattern, these simple blocks can
transform a design and create interesting secondary patterns. Each quilt uses
this concept differently, challenging you to approach color in a new way.
The Workshop for this section is Creative Fabric Selection. It will guide you in making
informed, confident color choices while keeping your own personal preferences in mind.

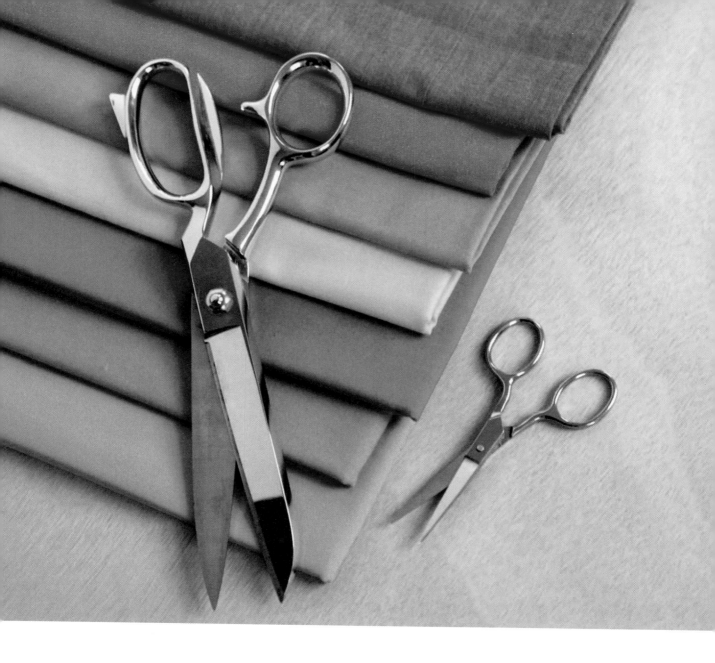

I have found that color is a very personal thing; we all have different experiences or knowledge that affects how we feel about color. While one color brings up a positive memory, another could bring up a bad memory. Consider what colors you are drawn to and why. Sometimes we like colors for their practicality. For example, I cannot stop buying gray sweaters. I am fond of gray, but more importantly, it goes with nearly everything else in my closet. Many of us make fabric selections in the same way and end up with a large stash of one or two favorite colors rather than a variety.

TIP Reorganizing your fabric stash is a fun opportunity to re-evaluate your fabric buying habits. It is also a good time to see what colors have been depleted or which colors you do not need to buy for a while.

Color and fabric selection are crucial to quilting. They have so much affect on the final look of a quilt. This is why it is so important to be able to look past the colors when viewing a quilt pattern. Colors are powerful; it can be difficult to see the possibility in a design if you do not like the colors or fabrics used. The easiest way to visualize how a quilt would look with other colors is to sketch it out. There are blank Quilt Coloring Book Pages featuring flat shots (see page 112) for each quilt in this book. These give you the freedom to play with different ideas before you ever cut into any fabric.

When making HSTs, color and fabric placement make a huge difference in the overall design. Since each HST is made up of two halves, the contrast between the two is important. Using two fabrics that have high contrast results in a very bold design. On the other hand, using two fabrics that have low contrast results in a subtle design. The three quilts in this chapter explore this concept.

WORKSHOP:
CREATIVE FABRIC SELECTION

While there is nothing wrong with using fabrics from a single fabric collection or designer in a project, choosing your own selection of fabrics adds a personalized twist. I believe the first step toward doing this successfully is to take a closer look at the different elements that make up a fabric print.

Analyzing Fabric

The first thing that most people see when they analyze a piece of fabric is the color. For some fabrics, determining the overall color is easy, while others are made up of many colors rather than a single dominant color.

Fabrics that feature a single color in multiple shades or with the addition of cream or white mix well with other fabrics. These types of fabrics are often called "blenders." The prints are generally small in scale, so they do not demand a lot of attention.

The next type of print you'll find is fabric with small accents of other colors. These fabrics still read overall as a single color, but have other competing colors as well. Depending on how large or small these accent colors are, it makes the print look busier.

Finally, there are focus fabrics. Focus fabrics have many colors in them and often do not read as one overall color. They are generally large in scale and feature all or most of the colors in a single fabric collection. These fabrics should be used sparingly together, depending on the overall look you are working toward. They are great to use as a starting point for a color scheme.

TIP When considering a fabric for a project, also take a look at the fabric's value. An easy way to analyze the various values of the fabrics in a selection is to take a black and white photo. This allows you to focus on the value of each print in relation to the other fabrics, then either work toward finding an even level of value or a balance of both light and dark.

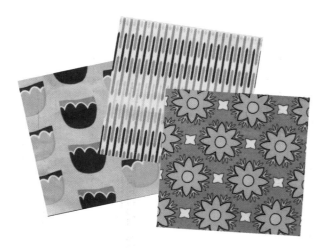

Pattern vs. Solids

Pattern is another main element of a fabric print. The three most common types are florals, geometrics, and novelty patterns. Patterns of the same type are easy to mix with one another. When mixing pattern types I recommend making sure there is a good balance.

The directionality of a fabric pattern is another thing to keep in mind when choosing fabrics. A pattern's direction can be one-way, two-way or multi-way.

Also be aware of pattern scale when choosing fabrics. Small-scale prints are easy to cut up and use as small pieces. Large-scale prints catch the eye, and are best

used in large pieces to avoid losing the design. On the other hand, chopping up large-scale prints can completely change the way the fabric looks, which is fun to experiment with.

Finally, we cannot leave out solids and semi-solids. These fabrics are the perfect addition to any fabric combination because they give the eye a place to rest. Try using all solids in a project to really let the colors and design shine. Mix a few solids in with a print fabric selection to calm down busier prints.

Color Schemes

When choosing fabrics for a project, I find it best to start with too many and then subtract. Make an initial pull without thinking too much, then analyze each print and determine whether it is adding to or detracting from the overall color scheme. If you get stuck, walk away for a few minutes or take a photo and ask a friend. Sometimes a different set of eyes will be able to spot the trouble print or color right away.

A great place to start looking for color schemes for your projects is right in your craft room. Start with a single piece of fabric or fabric collection and pull colors from it. Those original fabrics sometimes may not even end up in the final design, but will give you a place to start. Here are a few examples:

The Vast quilt (see page 51) uses solid colors pulled from my Geometric Bliss fabric collection.

This fabric selection was based on colors from a single fabric print.

This fabric selection was based on a photograph.

HSTs were one of the very first quilt blocks I ever tried, beyond simple patchwork squares. I was so intrigued by the symmetry and design possibilities they held. When I made my first two patchwork quilts, I saved all the little triangles that get cut off when making bias binding. I had no idea what I would do with them, but I couldn't throw them away. One day I decided to sew them together and make a small block. That block was the beginning of my love for HSTs and the inspiration for Opposites Attract.

This quilt explores one of my favorite aspects of color theory: warm and cool colors. The warm side of the color wheel covers red-purple through yellow, while the cool side covers yellow-green through purple. When grouped together and set next to one another, these colors create a subtle contrast that can be used to create all kinds of designs.

Finished HST Size: 5½"

Finished Quilt Size: 66" x 77"

Note: Use a ¼" seam allowance throughout.

FABRIC SELECTION TREATMENT I chose many different fabrics for this quilt, to give it a scrappy look. I was careful to select fabrics that were predominately one color, and that had minimal contrasting accents. For the warm colors, I selected a range of reds, oranges, and yellows, in a variety of shades. For the cool colors, I selected greens, blues, and purples, with a mix of light and dark prints.

MATERIALS

Warm fabrics:
1/4 yard of 14 fabrics

Cool fabrics:
1/4 yard of 14 fabrics

Backing fabric: 4³/₄ yards

Binding fabric: ⁵/₈ yard

Batting: 74" x 85"

TIP If you'd like to cut squares from scraps, you'll need a total of 84 squares from warm fabrics and 84 squares from cool fabrics.

Cutting

From each warm fabric, cut:
(1) 6¹/₂" x WOF strip, subcut strip into
(6) 6¹/₂" squares

From each cool fabric, cut:
(1) 6¹/₂" x WOF strip, subcut strip into
(6) 6¹/₂" squares

From binding fabric, cut:
(8) 2¹/₂" x WOF strips

Assemble HSTs

1. Keep warm squares and cool squares separated. Construct 168 HSTs using the two-at-a-time method (see page 15), pairing a warm square with a cool square.

2. Press seams toward the cool fabrics. Trim HSTs to 6" square.

TIP Use a large plastic storage container or a paper grocery bag to mix up squares when piecing. This makes pairing up squares more random and gives your HSTs plenty of variety.

Assemble Quilt Top

1. Referring to Figure 1, arrange HSTs in 14 rows of 12 blocks each. Sew HSTs in each row together. Press seams in one direction, alternating direction every other row.

2. Sew rows together. Press the seams open.

Finishing

1. Cut backing yardage in half. Press. Trim off the selvages and sew pieces together lengthwise. Press the seam open.

2. Baste and quilt as desired. Bind using your preferred method.

QUILTING TREATMENT
For Opposites Attract, I chose to free-motion quilt the warm and cool sections differently to increase the contrast between them. The warm sections are quilted with dense organic lines, and the cool sections are quilted with my signature doodle loops.

VARIATION
It is easy to modify the Opposites Attract design by arranging the HSTs in different layouts. The chevron design of my quilt is one of many options. Lay the entire quilt out on the floor or on a design wall to make it easier to visualize.

Figure 1

Playing with color placement and HSTs opens up a lot of really fun design possibilities. Modifying the colors can have a large effect on the overall look of a quilt—especially with Interlocked. The specific arrangement of the colors in this quilt creates the secondary shapes, in this case diamonds and larger triangles. If the colors were arranged differently, these elements would be lost.

This quilt is put together in rows. Each row has a certain order and it is not until the quilt top is finished that the secondary shapes appear. It is important to pay close attention to piecing when working on this quilt, so that blocks do not get out of order or oriented incorrectly. I recommend piecing one row at a time, to avoid errors.

Finished HST Size: 5½"

Finished Quilt Size: 49½" x 66"

Note: Use a ¼" seam allowance throughout.

FABRIC SELECTION TREATMENT For Interlocked I started with an analogous color scheme of green, blue, and purple. I deviated from this slightly by leaving out a true blue and using a green-blue instead. I kept the values of all three colors very even across my fabric seletions. This helps minimize distraction from the design.

MATERIALS

Fabric A (greens): 1⅛ yards total

Fabric B (purples): 1⅛ yards total

Fabric C (blues): 1⅛ yards total

Backing fabric: 3¼ yards

Binding fabric: ½ yard

Batting: 57½" x 74"

///// **TIP** If you'd like to cut squares from scraps, you'll need 36 squares each from Fabrics A, B, and C.

Cutting

From Fabric A, cut:
(6) 6½" x WOF strips, subcut each strip into (6) 6½" squares

From Fabric B, cut:
(6) 6½" x WOF strips, subcut each strip into (6) 6½" squares

From Fabric C, cut:
(6) 6½" x WOF strips, subcut each strip into (6) 6½" squares

From binding fabric, cut:
(6) 2½" x WOF strips

Assemble HSTs

Use the two-at-a-time method (see page 15) to construct all HSTs.

1. Construct 36 HSTs using 18 Fabric A squares and 18 Fabric B squares. Press seams open. Trim HSTs to 6" square.

2. Construct 36 HSTs using 18 Fabric A squares and 18 Fabric C squares.

Press the seams open. Trim HSTs to 6" square.

3. Construct 36 HSTs using 18 Fabric B squares and 18 Fabric C squares. Press seams open. Trim HSTs to 6" square.

Assemble Rows

1. Referring to Figure 1, construct Rows 1 and 10, using 9 Fabric A/B blocks in each row.

2. Referring to Figure 2, construct Rows 4 and 7, using 9 Fabric A/B blocks in each row.

3. Referring to Figure 3, construct Rows 6 and 9, using 9 Fabric A/C blocks in each row.

4. Referring to Figure 4, construct Rows 3 and 12, using 9 Fabric A/C blocks in each row.

5. Referring to Figure 5, construct Rows 2 and 5, using 9 Fabric B/C blocks in each row.

6. Referring to Figure 6, construct Rows 8 and 11, using 9 Fabric B/C blocks in each row.

///// **TIP** Label each row as you go to keep things organized and easy to put together. A piece of masking tape or simply a scrap of paper and a pin work well.

Assemble Quilt Top

1. Referring to Figure 7, arrange rows in numerical order. Press seams in one direction, alternating direction every other row.

2. Sew rows together. Press the seams open.

Finishing

1. Cut backing yardage in half. Press. Trim off the selvages and sew pieces together lengthwise. Press the seam open.

2. Baste and quilt as desired. Bind using your preferred method.

QUILTING TREATMENT
For Interlocked, I wanted the quilting to blend into the top, so as not to interfere with the overall design. I quilted it with long chains of doodle loops.

VARIATION
Experiment with value and color in this quilt to adjust the contrast. Higher contrast in value between the three colors will make the shapes more distinct.

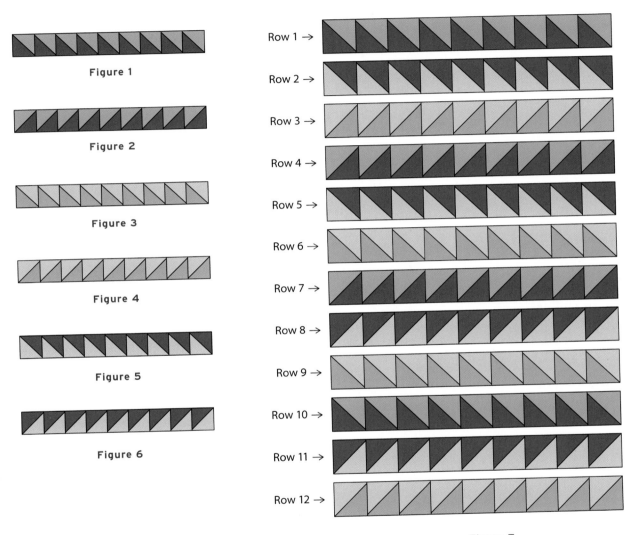

Figure 1

Figure 2

Figure 3

Figure 4

Figure 5

Figure 6

Row 1 →
Row 2 →
Row 3 →
Row 4 →
Row 5 →
Row 6 →
Row 7 →
Row 8 →
Row 9 →
Row 10 →
Row 11 →
Row 12 →

Figure 7

RADIANT

While I love color just as much (or more!) than the next person, I also enjoy working without color. A simple black and white color scheme is very striking, because the contrast between black and white is at a maximum. It is a timeless, classic color scheme that is used across mediums from quilting and fashion to fine art and decor. On top of that, black and white fabric prints are fun to collect and can generally be found in abundance. You'll find them stocked in both modern and traditional quilt shops.

This quilt features four large blocks with rotational symmetry. This means that whichever way the block is turned the design does not change. The HSTs seem to be "radiating" toward the center — all thanks to color placement and HST arrangement.

Finished HST Size: 4"

Finished Block Size: 16"

Finished Quilt Size: 64" x 64"

Note: Use a ¹⁄₄" seam allowance throughout.

FABRIC SELECTION TREATMENT I couldn't resist using a rainbow of colors to complement the black and white prints. I narrowed my scheme down to eight colors and two types of black and white prints. About a half of my black and white prints are predominately white, and the rest are predominately black. This adds some variety and breaks up the design to keep things interesting.

MATERIALS

Block fabric(s):
¼ yard each of 13 fabrics

Background fabric(s):
¼ yard each of 13 fabrics

Backing fabric: 4 yards

Binding fabric: ½ yard

Batting: 72" x 72"

Cutting

From each block fabric, cut:
(5) 7¼" squares, for a total of
64 squares

From each background fabric, cut:
(5) 7¼" squares, for a total of
64 squares

From binding fabric, cut:
(7) 2½" x WOF strips

Assemble HSTs and Blocks

1. Construct 256 HSTs using the four-at-a-time method (page 16), pairing a block fabric square with a background fabric square. Press seams open. Trim HSTs to 4½" square.

2. Each block is made up of 16 HSTs. Arrange HSTs into 4 rows of 4 blocks each **(Fig. 1)**. Sew HSTs in each row together. Press seams in one direction, alternating direction every other row. Sew rows together. Press seams open. Repeat to create a total of 16 blocks.

Assemble Quilt Top

1. Referring to Figure 2, arrange blocks in 4 rows of 4 blocks each. Press seams in one direction, alternating direction every other row.

2. Sew rows together. Press the seams open.

Finishing

1. Cut backing yardage in half. Press. Trim off the selvages and sew pieces together lengthwise. Press the seam open.

2. Baste and quilt as desired. Bind using your preferred method.

QUILTING TREATMENT

Radiant was quilted by longarm quilter Melissa Kelley. I chose a geometric square allover design to complement the graphic fabrics and bold contrast.

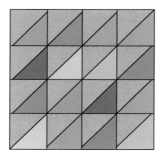

Figure 1

VARIATION

A fun way to add excitement to a black and white color scheme is with a pop of color. From using a single color accent to a whole range of colors, there is a lot of room to experiment. Try flipping around the smaller blocks so that the colors meet in the center for a twist on the design.

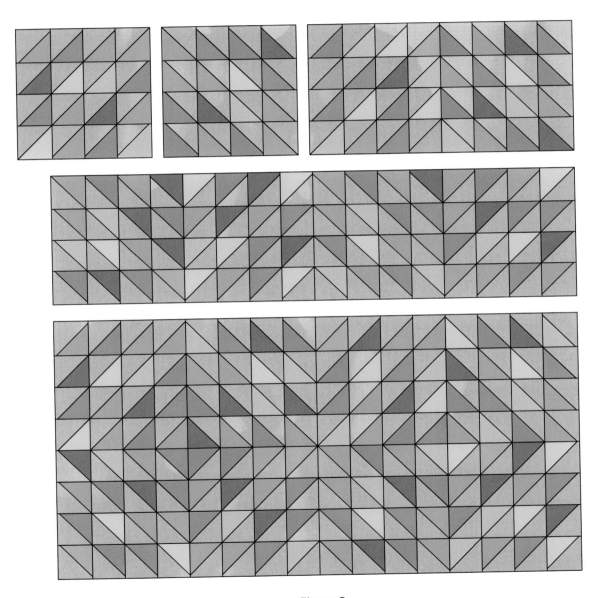

Figure 2

Relative Scale

CHAPTER 2

What exactly is scale? Scale is the relative size of one thing
compared to another. As quilters, we often think about scale
in terms of fabric prints, but scale in the piecing and design of a quilt
is just as important. The three quilts in this chapter play with the idea
of scale through super-sizing a block beyond its expected use, using a variety
of finished block sizes in one pattern and even using smaller blocks to create
BIG secondary designs. The Workshop walks you through Resizing a Quilt Pattern,
making it easy to tailor any pattern to any size you wish to create.

Scale is generally the first element that I alter when I am in the beginning stages of designing a new pattern. It is a fun way to explore a concept, and it is generally a pretty straightforward process. There are a lot of different reasons why you should consider scale when starting a project. I usually ask myself a few questions to help me make decisions about scale: What kind of mood do I want to evoke? What kinds of fabrics am I using? Do I want the project to be a specific size? How much time do I have?

Some questions are answered more easily than others. If I am crunched for time and need to finish a quilt quickly, I might choose larger scale blocks to speed things along. If time is not a consideration, I might use smaller blocks. When I need a quilt to be a specific size, the scale is some-times based on the math. For example, if I am designing a 24" square mini quilt, I would not choose 10" blocks, since 24 is not easily divisible by 10. A single block or four standard 12" blocks would be more appropriate.

Oftentimes the fabric helps to determine the scale of a design. When I want the fabrics to be the focal point of the

quilt, a design with large uncut sections will keep the focus on the fabrics. This holds true if the fabrics are also large in scale. While it can be fun to chop up large-scale prints, if I want to preserve that print, I will keep the piecing large-scale too. Mood is another thing to consider when determining scale. Large-scale designs often feel more bold and graphic than small-scale projects.

WORKSHOP:
RESIZING A QUILT PATTERN

Resizing a quilt pattern can seem like a daunting task if you are not comfortable with math. Honestly though, it just takes a little practice to get the hang of it. It is a great skill to have, because not every pattern will suit your needs. I am going to show you two different ways to resize patterns in this book, using Opposites Attract (see page 35) as an example.

This is a block-based quilt pattern in a simple grid layout, which are the easiest types of patterns to resize. Each HST block measures 5½" finished, the overall quilt size is 66" x 77", and the blocks are arranged in 14 rows of 12 blocks each. We want to resize this quilt to approximately 84" x 92" to fit a queen-size bed. The two different methods of resizing are adding blocks and changing the size of the blocks.

Adding or Subtracting Blocks

This is the simplest method of resizing a quilt pattern. Work with the finished size of the blocks listed in the pattern directions when doing calculations. This leaves the finished block and cutting sizes unchanged. In this case, our finished block size is 5½".

First, we want to figure out how many 5½" finished blocks we need to achieve a width of 84". So, 84" divided by 5½" equals 15.27 blocks. We do not want a partial block, so let's round up to 16 blocks. Keeping the number of blocks in each row even, ensures that the zig-zag design in this quilt is kept complete. Now we can find our actual quilt width: 16 blocks multiplied by 5½" equals 88" wide.

Next, we want to determine how many 5½" finished blocks we need to achieve a length of 92". This is calculated the same way as the width, that is 92" divided by 5½" equals 16.73 blocks. This rounds up to 17. So, 17 blocks multiplied by 5½" gives us an overall length of 93½".

To get a quilt that is 88" x 93½", we need 16 blocks across and 17 blocks down. This gets us close to our desired size, without too much hassle.

Here are some helpful methods to use when working through this type of resizing:

Desired width of quilt: _____

Desired length of quilt: _____

Finished block size: _____

Number of blocks across =
desired width of quilt / finished block size

Actual width of quilt =
number of blocks across x finished block size

Number of blocks down =
desired length of quilt / finished block size

Actual length of quilt =
number of blocks down x finished block size

Changing the Size of the Blocks

The other way to approach resizing a quilt is to change the size of the blocks. When resizing blocks, you always want to work from the finished block size, rather than the unfinished size. (The unfinished size simply includes the seam allowance.) Again, we want to make a queen-size quilt, approximately 84" x 92". Before we do any calculations, we need to decide which measurement is more important. Since we are working with square blocks in a rectangular layout, we may not be able to achieve the exact dimensions. For this example, I am going to make the width of 84" the priority. Because we are keeping the block arrangement of 14 rows of 12 blocks, we are going to use those numbers to determine our finished block size.

Let's see how large our blocks need to be to achieve a width of 84". So, 84" divided by 12 blocks equals 7" finished blocks.

The length is calculated in the same way: 7" finished blocks multiplied by 14 equals 98". So, we have a finished quilt size of 84" x 98", with 7" finished blocks. You can now use one of the charts in the Techniques section (see page 12) to determine what size to cut squares based on your desired construction method.

Desired width of quilt: _____

Desired length of quilt: _____

Number of blocks across: _____

Number of blocks down: _____

Finished block size =
desired width of quilt / number of blocks across

Width of quilt =
finished block size x number of blocks across

Length of quilt =
finished block size x number of blocks down

TIP If you're working with a pattern that has large blocks made from multiple units, such as Woven (see page 61), treat those large blocks as a single block to keep them intact when resizing. Once those are resized, you can determine the size of the smaller blocks.

VAST

My favorite way to experiment with scale is super-sizing. This concept is really simple: take a single block or design and blow it up. I began experimenting with this technique as I was searching the Internet for inspiration a few summers back. I came across an article featuring barn quilts from around the country. If you are not familiar with them, barn quilts are painted quilt blocks, usually on metal or wood that are affixed to barns or buildings. They are generally pretty large, so that they are easily seen from the road.

I loved the idea of using a single large-scale block as an entire quilt and had to make one right away. I started with a traditional 12" starflower block design, and scaled the finished HST size up to 17" from 3". The Giant Vintage Star Quilt was born, and so was my curiosity for super-sized quilts! Another great thing about large-scale quilts is they are super fast. I cut, pieced, quilted, and bound that first quilt in 24 hours.

FABRIC SELECTION TREATMENT For the Vast quilt, rather than working from a quilt block design, I let color be the guide to this random arrangement of HSTs. This is a great design to show off a unique color scheme, or your favorite fabrics.

Finished HST Size: 17"

Finished Quilt Size: 68" x 68"

Note: Use a 1/4" seam allowance throughout

MATERIALS

Block fabrics: ½ yard each of 8 fabrics

Backing fabric: 4¼ yards

Binding fabric: ½ yard

Batting: 76" x 76"

TIP Working with large pieces of fabric can be tricky. It can be difficult to make accurate cuts, and the fabric can easily stretch out of shape. On top of that, inaccuracies in large piecing tend to be more obvious. Before cutting, I like to treat my fabric with a spray starch alternative. This makes the fabric easier to cut and helps keep it in shape once I am handling it. It is tempting to speed stitch across long seams, but slowing down will help keep those seams straight and even. A ¼" foot and seam guides are both great tools to ensure accurate seams.

Cutting

From each block fabric, cut: (2) 18" squares, for a total of 16 squares

From binding fabric, cut: (7) 2½" x WOF strips

Assemble HSTs

1. Construct 16 HSTs using the two-at-a-time method (see page 15). Press seams open. Trim HSTs to 17½" square.

TIP A standard 24" acrylic ruler is not long enough to mark and cut apart these giant HSTs. I like to extend mine by temporarily attaching a 6" square ruler to one end with masking tape.

Assemble Quilt Top

1. Referring to Figure 1, arrange blocks into 4 rows of 4 HSTs each. Sew HSTs in each row together. Press seams to the side, alternating the direction every other row.

2. Sew rows together. Press the seams open.

Finishing

1. Cut backing yardage in half. Press. Trim off the selvages and sew pieces together lengthwise. Press the seam open.

2. Baste and quilt as desired. Bind using your preferred method.

QUILTING TREATMENT

Vast was quilted by longarm quilter Melissa Kelley. She quilted each HST half separately. There are a total of eight different designs, one for each color. The dense quilting and intricate designs give extra interest to an all-solids quilt.

VARIATION

Creating your own super-sized HST design is simple. Begin by choosing a four-by-four block design, including any of the blocks featured in the Block Party section (see page 82). Replace half the squares (and yardage) used in Vast with a single background fabric. Create the HSTs and arrange them in your desired design.

Figure 1

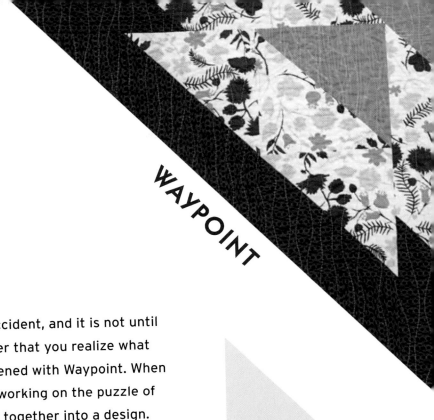

Often designs come about by accident, and it is not until you go back to study them closer that you realize what inspired you. That is what happened with Waypoint. When I was designing it, I was simply working on the puzzle of fitting three different size HSTs together into a design. Looking back, I can see inspiration from two types of quilt designs that I have long admired: medallion and mariner's compass.

Medallion quilts typically have a focal center design, which is surrounded by ever growing and changing borders. Mariner's compass quilts often feature a large centralized block in the styling of a compass. Waypoint pulls in elements from both. It is built from the center out, starting with a central block, and gradually expanded using borders. It is not until the quilt is complete that you can see the compass. The final border reveals a compass made from dark purple in my version.

Finished HST Sizes: 3", 6", 9"

Finished Quilt Size: 54" x 54"

Note: Use a 1/4" seam allowance throughout.

FABRIC SELECTION TREATMENT I chose two groups of color for this quilt. The first is the eggplant and dark fuchsia group. To make this design really pop, I then chose colors on the other side of the color wheel, red-orange and a warm vanilla. The contrast these two groups creates gives this quilt a little extra punch. Think about the relationship amongst the colors when choosing your palette. Or, play with different values of the same color for a monochromatic look.

MATERIALS

Fabric A (fuchsia): ¾ yard

Fabric B (orange): 1 yard

Fabric C (vanilla): 1 yard

Fabric D (purple): ¾ yard

Backing fabric: 3½ yards

Binding fabric: ½ yard

Batting: 62" x 62"

Cutting

From Fabric A, cut:
(1) 10" x WOF strip, subcut strip into
(2) 10" squares and (2) 4" squares

(2) 7" x WOF strips, subcut strips into
(10) 7" squares

From Fabric B, cut:
(2) 10" x WOF strips, subcut one
strip into (4) 10" squares. Subcut
remaining strip into (2) 10" squares
and (8) 4" squares

(1) 7" x WOF strip, subcut strip into
(6) 7" squares

From Fabric C, cut:
(2) 10" x WOF strips, subcut strips
into (8) 10" squares

(1) 7" x WOF strip, subcut strip into
(6) 7" squares

(1) 4" x WOF strip, subcut strip into
(6) 4" squares

From Fabric D, cut:
(1) 10" x WOF strip, subcut strip into
(4) 10" squares

(2) 7" x WOF strips, subcut strips into
(10) 7" squares

From binding fabric, cut:
(6) 2½" x WOF strips

TIP Make yourself a cheat sheet with a swatch of each fabric and a label to minimize mistakes while constructing all the different HSTs.

Assemble HSTs

Use the two-at-a-time method (see page 15) to construct all HSTs.

1. Construct 4 HSTs using (2) 10" Fabric A squares and (2) 10" Fabric B squares. Press seams open. Trim HSTs to 9½" square.

2. Construct 8 HSTs using (4) 7" Fabric A squares and (4) 7" Fabric B squares. Press seams open. Trim HSTs to 6½" square.

3. Construct 4 HSTs using (2) 4" Fabric A squares and (2) 4" Fabric B squares. Press seams open. Trim HSTs to 3½" square.

4. Construct 8 HSTs using (4) 10" Fabric B squares and (4) 10" Fabric C squares. Press seams open. Trim HSTs to 9½" square.

5. Construct 4 HSTs using (2) 7" Fabric B squares and (2) 7" Fabric C squares. Press seams open. Trim HSTs to 6½" square.

6. Construct 12 HSTs using (6) 4" Fabric B squares and (6) 4" Fabric C squares. Press seams open. Trim HSTs to 3½" square.

7. Construct 8 HSTs using (4) 10" Fabric C squares and (4) 10" Fabric D squares. Press seams open. Trim HSTs to 9½" square.

8. Construct 8 HSTs using (4) 7" Fabric C squares and (4) 7" Fabric D squares. Press seams open. Trim HSTs to 6½" square.

9. Construct 12 HSTs using (6) 7" Fabric A squares and (6) 7" Fabric D squares. Press seams open. Trim HSTs to 6½" square.

Assemble Borders

Border 1

1. For left and right borders, sew (2) 6½" Fabric A/B HSTs together **(Fig. 1)**. Press seams open. Create 2 units.

2. For top and bottom borders, sew (2) 6½" Fabric A/B HSTs together. On either end, sew a 6½" Fabric A/D HST **(Fig. 2)**. Press seams open. Create 2 units.

Border 2

1. For left and right borders, sew (2) 6½" Fabric C/D and (2) 6½" Fabric A/D HSTs together **(Fig. 3)**. Press seams open. Create 2 units.

2. For top and bottom borders, sew (2) 6½" Fabric C/D and (2) 6½" Fabric A/D HSTs together. On either end, sew a 6½" Fabric B/C HST **(Fig. 4)**. Press seams open. Create 2 units.

Border 3

1. For left and right borders, sew (2) 9½" Fabric C/D and (2) 9½" Fabric B/C HSTs together. Press seams open. Create 2 units **(Fig. 5)**.

2. For top and bottom borders, sew (2) 9½" Fabric C/D and (2) 9½" Fabric B/C HSTs together. On either end, sew a 9½" Fabric A/B HST **(Fig. 6)**. Press the seams open. Create 2 units.

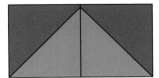

Figure 1

Figure 2

Figure 3

Figure 4

Figure 5

Figure 6

VARIATION

The sizes of the blocks in Waypoint were designed so that each round fits nicely together. At the very center point of the quilt, a central 12" block made of 3" HSTs starts the quilt. The next two borders are made of 6" blocks. The final border is 9". If you wanted to make this quilt larger, the next border would be another round of 9" blocks. Beyond that you'd add two borders of 12" blocks.

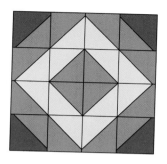

Figure 7

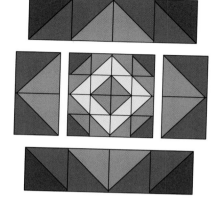

Figure 8

Figure 9

Assemble Quilt Top

1. Arrange (16) 3½" HSTs into 4 rows of 4 blocks each **(Fig. 7)**. Sew HSTs in each row together. Press seams in one direction, alternating direction every other row. Sew rows together. Press seams open.

2. Sew the left and right Border 1's to the sides of the center block **(Fig. 8)**. Press seams open. Sew the top and bottom Border 1's to the top and bottom of the center block. Press seams open.

3. Referring to Figures 9 and 10, continue to sew the borders to the center unit, starting with the left and right borders and then the top and bottom borders. Press all the seams open.

Finishing

1. Cut backing yardage in half. Press. Trim off the selvages and sew pieces together lengthwise. Press the seam open.

2. Baste and quilt as desired. Bind using your preferred method.

QUILTING TREATMENT

Waypoint has a lot of sharpness to it, because of the design and color contrast. To give it a little sofness, I quilted it with wavy organic lines using my walking foot. Gently turn the quilt back and forth while stitching to get a nice even wave.

Figure 10

In the last few years I have taken up knitting as a hobby. At first, I feared it would take too much time away from my quilt making. What I didn't expect is that it would soon influence my quilt designs. Knitting is a much slower process than quilting, and while working stitch by stitch to create the fabric of a shawl, I began to see quilt design possibilities. Woven is one of the designs born of my knitting. It may be tough to see at first glance, but if you look closely, the larger blocks create a woven design. My knitting may have inspired this quilt, but it has roots in traditional quilt design as well. Traditional Ocean Waves blocks feature a similar design made from hundreds of tiny HSTs. While there are still plenty of small HSTs in this quilt for those who enjoy working with smaller units, the inclusion of a few larger HSTs adds interest and plays with that s cale we are looking to achieve.

FABRIC SELECTION TREATMENT Jewel tones are the star of Woven, with cool indigo, turquoise, purple, fuchsia, and a pop of pink, all on a background of white. It is a subdued palette, but there is still plenty of contrast to show off the pattern. I chose primarily blenders for this quilt, to keep the prints from distracting from the overall design.

Finished HST Sizes: 2½", 5"

Finished Block Size: 20"

Finished Quilt Size: 60" x 80"

Note: Use a ¼" seam allowance throughout.

MATERIALS

Fabric A: 1 yard

Fabric B: 1 yard

Fabric C: 1 yard

Fabric D: 1 yard

Background fabric: 3 yards

Backing fabric: 5 yards

Binding fabric: ⁵/₈ yard

Batting: 68" x 88"

Cutting

From Fabric A, cut:
(1) 12" x WOF strip, subcut strip into (3) 12" squares

(2) 7" x WOF strips, subcut strips into (12) 7" squares

From Fabric B, cut:
(1) 12" x WOF strip, subcut strip into (3) 12" squares

(2) 7" x WOF strips, subcut strips into (12) 7" squares

From Fabric C, cut:
(1) 12" x WOF strip, subcut strip into (3) 12" squares

(2) 7" x WOF strips, subcut strips into (12) 7" squares

From Fabric D, cut:
(1) 12" x WOF strip, subcut strip into (3) 12" squares

(2) 7" x WOF strips, subcut strips into (12) 7" squares

From background fabric, cut:
(4) 12" x WOF strips, subcut strips into (12) 12" squares

(8) 7" x WOF strips, subcut strips into (48) 7" squares

From binding fabric, cut:
(8) 2½" x WOF strips

Assemble HSTs

Use the eight-at-a-time method (see page 17) to construct all HSTs.

1. Construct 96 HSTs pairing 12" Fabric A, B, C, and D squares with 12" background squares. Press seams toward prints. Trim HSTs to 5½" square.

2. Construct 384 HSTs pairing 7" Fabric A, B, C, and D squares with 7" background squares. Press seams toward prints. Trim HSTs to 3" square.

TIP Working in an assembly-line fashion for large quilts is efficient but can be tiring. Keep things interesting and avoid straining yourself by sewing, pressing, and trimming sets of 40–80 HSTs at a time. This will help you steer clear of having to trim all those HSTs at once.

Assemble Blocks

Each block is made up of 4 pairs of matching 5½" HSTs and (32) 3" HSTs.

1. Sew 3" HSTs into (8) 4-patch blocks **(Fig. 1)**. Press seams in one direction, alternating direction every other row. Press the remaining seam open.

2. Sew 4-patch blocks and a pair of 5½" HSTs together **(Fig. 2)**. Press seams in one direction, alternating direction every other row. Press the remaining seam open.

3. Sew 4 units from Step 2 together to create a single block **(Fig. 3)**. Press seams in one direction, alternating direction every other row. Press the remaining seam open.

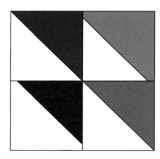

Figure 1

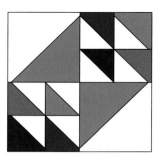

Figure 2

Figure 3

Assemble Quilt Top

1. Referring to Figure 4, arrange blocks in 4 rows of 3 blocks each. Press seams in one direction, alternating direction every other row.

2. Sew rows together. Press the seams open.

Finishing

1. Cut backing yardage in half. Press. Trim off the selvages and sew pieces together lengthwise. Press the seam open.

2. Baste and quilt as desired. Bind using your preferred method.

QUILTING TREATMENT

Woven was quilted by longarm quilter Melissa Kelley. Since there is a lot going on in the piecing of this quilt, I wanted to keep it simple with an allover quilting design. I chose a curvy popcorn pattern to contrast with the geometric design of the quilt.

VARIATION

I can picture many different color palettes that would look beautiful in this design. Experiment with the woven effect by increasing or decreasing the number of colors used. A two-color palette would be a very striking choice, or dig into your scrap bin and let loose the entire rainbow.

Figure 4

CHAPTER 3

Patchwork Play

There is something so magical about simple patchwork. It instantly
makes a project feel handmade, which I love. In this chapter,
I encourage you to replace a single piece of fabric with a pieced unit and
incorporate patchwork into your HST creations. Each quilt in this chapter
challenges you to look beyond the basic HST design and take it one step further.
Let loose and play with these techniques to create something special. This Workshop
reviews Scrap Quilting, which is one of the most fun ways to incorporate pieced
components into your work (and economical too!).

It can be difficult to let go of mistakes when they are still fresh. I have done my fair share of sulking over things not lining up or a tuck or two in the back of a quilt. Thankfully, all that is needed to fix most of those things is time. After a while, those issues become less obvious because we simply forget about them.

Quilting offers us many opportunities to think outside of the box. Whether it is through a mistake or lack of materials, problem solving can lead to great ideas. That is the beauty of making things; you get to make all the decisions. I think this can be hard for non-makers to understand. Yes, it would be cheaper and more efficient to purchase a ready-made quilt from a big box store, but the advantage of making a quilt yourself is the ability to make something unique. It's fun to have so many options, and to create new ones through experimentation.

After I made my fair share of HSTs, I was ready to bend the rules a little and take my favorite block a step further. Simple patchwork is one of my absolute favorite things in quilting, so it only seemed right to try incorporating it into HSTs. Instead of using two single fabrics to create an HST, I substituted one of those fabrics with a sewn block. Different blocks or combinations produce different results. This opens up a whole new world of HST possibilities. I have only scratched the surface with the quilts in this chapter. There are so many other ways to explore this idea.

WORKSHOP:
SCRAP QUILTING

Scraps, we all have them. Making only a quilt or two can result in a lot of leftover scraps. I'm pretty sure they multiply when our backs are turned! Everyone has their own preferences for what kinds of scraps are saved, organized and used. I have developed a few habits over the years and want to pass on these great tips for maximizing your scraps for making HSTs.

What Is a Scrap?

What is considered a scrap varies a lot depending on whom you ask. Some quilters save any piece larger than $1/2$" square, while others would consider anything smaller than a fat quarter (18" x 22") a scrap. I fall somewhere in between the two. If it is a really precious piece of fabric, I'll save tiny pieces, but I generally do not save anything smaller than approximately 2" square. If a piece is larger than a standard 12" quilt block, I fold it up and keep it with the rest of my fabrics. Everything else ends up in my scrap bins.

TIP Tired of working with your own scraps? Organize a scrap swap between friends. If you're overwhelmed with your stash of scraps, pay it forward: pass them on to a new quilter who may not have many scraps to work with.

Scrap Storage

There are many different ways to store scraps. The trick is to find a system that works for you. I switch back and forth between sorting by color and sorting by pattern type. I currently have my scraps separated into three types: solids, blenders, and focus fabrics. I also have a separate stash of special fabric scraps, vintage fabric scraps, and binding scraps.

If you precut your scraps before storing, that gives you another storage option. Planning a few scrap projects in advance will give you some insight into what kinds of scrap sizes are most useful to you. Typically, squares in various sizes and strips are the easiest to use. To keep things under control, consider cutting scraps into specific sizes after you finish a project. Soon you'll have enough for a whole new project and the cutting is already done. Precutting scraps is an easy way to collect squares for the quilts in this book. You'll find square sizes and totals in the cutting instructions for each project.

Create Your Own "Scrap Fabric"

A great way to use up scraps and give a project a new twist is to create your own "scrap fabric." Piece together scraps into large blocks of fabric and then cut it up into the squares for your project. This works great with strips too. A whole quilt made this way may seem a little overwhelming; a pillow or mini quilt is a great way to test out a time-consuming technique.

Do not be afraid to use multiple prints for a single fabric requirement. If a pattern calls for a certain color, mix it up by using a variety of scraps from fabrics in that color. If you do not have the appropriate scraps, cut a few squares out of some new fabric. It is an easy way to get a scrappy look without using scraps.

TIP Invest in a few acrylic rulers in smaller sizes for cutting up scraps. I get a lot of use out of my $6\frac{1}{2}$" square and my $3\frac{1}{2}$" and $18\frac{1}{2}$" rulers too.

Even if it does not strike your fancy, the important thing that scrap quilting can provide is its carefree attitude. Working with scraps gives you permission to break the rules. The point is: you make your own rules. If you want to use two different colors for the background, or a print, or five prints, you can. Do not feel limited by the choices I have made for my quilts; think of them more as a place to start your own quilt-making journey.

CITRUS PEEL

I don't know what it is about them, but string blocks have always appealed to me. I'll be the first to admit that I am not much of a scrap quilter, but I do tend to add scrap projects to my to-do list on a regular basis. To be honest, they intimidate me. They're time-consuming and generally require a lot of tedious cutting and piecing. I know my fear stems from the risk of having to abandon a project and admit defeat.

I am here to tell you, if you are afraid of scraps, this is the quilt for you. I was pretty anxious about making this quilt, and that anxiety was all for nothing. Paper piecing makes Citrus Peel come together so smoothly, and it has become one of my favorite quilts. Not only that, I really enjoyed making it!

Finished HST Size: 7½"

Finished Block Size: 15"

Finished Quilt Size: 60" x 75"

Note: Use a ¼" seam allowance throughout.

FABRIC SELECTION TREATMENT I focused on one main color for Citrus Peel, and added a few accent colors based on an analogous color scheme. Peach is the central color, in varying shades with pops of light and dark coral, yellow-orange, and gold. These colors are so cheerful and fresh; they are really enjoyable to work with. The peach solid for the background keeps the scheme soft and ties all the fabrics together.

MATERIALS

Block fabrics: ¼ yard each of 20 fabrics

Background fabric: 2½ yards

Backing fabric: 4 yards

Binding fabric: ½ yard

Batting: 68" x 83"

40 sheets of 8½" x 11" 20# copy paper

Glue stick

TIP If you'd like to cut strips from scraps, you'll need (80) strips 2" wide in each of the following lengths: 12½", 10", 8", and 4".

Cutting

From each block fabric, cut:
(4) 2" x WOF strips. Subcut (2) strips into (4) 12½" x 2" strips and (4) 8" x 2" strips. Subcut remaining (2) strips into (4) 10" x 2" strips and (4) 4" x 2" strips.

From background fabric, cut:
(10) 8½" x WOF strips, subcut strips into (40) 8½" squares

From binding fabric, cut:
(7) 2½" x WOF strips

Assemble String Blocks

1. Trim copy paper down to 8½" square. Using a pencil and a ruler, draw a single diagonal line from one corner to another.

TIP Save rotary blades that are too dull to cut fabric and pair them with standard acrylic quilting rulers to easily cut paper for paper piecing.

2. Sew 2 different 12½" strips together along the long edges, then press the seam open. Repeat with the remaining 12½" strips to construct a total of 40 pairs.

3. Apply a thin line of glue along the diagonal line of an 8½" square of paper. Carefully lay a 12½" pair right sides up on the glue, lining up the seam with the pencil line **(Fig. 1)**. Press in place with your fingers. Repeat with the remaining paper and pairs.

TIP When paper piecing, shorten your stitch length to make the paper easier to rip out when the blocks are finished.

4. Pin a 10" strip to one side of the center pair to start building the block. Be sure that the strip goes beyond the paper on each side **(Fig. 2)**. Sew in place, then press strip open **(Fig. 3)**. Repeat for the remaining blocks.

5. Pin an 8" strip to the 10" strip sewn in step 4, ensuring that the strip goes beyond the paper on each side. Sew in place, then press strip open. Repeat for the remaining blocks.

6. Pin a 4" strip to the 8" strip sewn in Step 5. Again, be sure that the strip goes beyond the paper on each

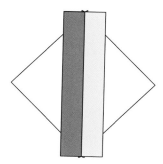

Figure 1

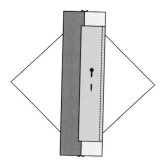

Figure 2

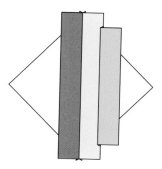

Figure 3

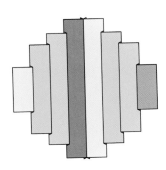

Figure 4

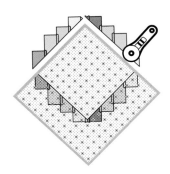

Figure 5

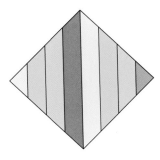

Figure 6

side. Sew in place, then press the strip open. Repeat for the remaining blocks.

7. Repeat Steps 4–6 on the other side to complete each block **(Fig. 4)**.

8. Using the paper as a guide, trim blocks to 8½" square **(Fig. 5)**. Leave the paper in place for now.

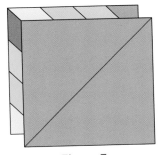

Figure 7

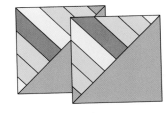

Figure 8

Assemble HSTs and Blocks

1. Construct 80 HSTs using the two-at-a-time method (see page 15), pairing a string block with a background fabric square. Press seams open **(Fig. 7)**.

2. Press the trimmed HSTs with spray starch to help avoid stretching. Trim HSTs to 8" square **(Fig. 8)**. Carefully remove the paper from the back of each block.

3. Sew the HSTs into (20) 4-patch blocks. Press all seams open **(Fig. 9)**.

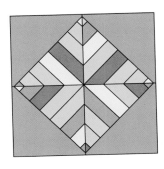

Figure 9

Assemble Quilt Top

1. Referring to Figure 10, arrange blocks into 5 rows of 4 blocks each. Press seams in one direction, alternating direction every other row.

2. Sew rows together. Press the seams open.

Finishing

1. Cut backing yardage in half. Press. Trim off the selvages and sew pieces together lengthwise. Press the seam open.

2. Baste and quilt as desired. Bind using your preferred method.

QUILTING TREATMENT

Citrus Peel was quilted by long-arm quilter Melissa Kelley. I knew the negative space created by the background fabric needed a special treatment. Melissa quilted a swirl and bubble crosses in the negative space and accentuated the string portions with feather-like waves.

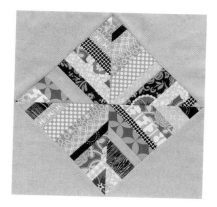

VARIATION

The string blocks outlined in this pattern are all made with 2" strips, but I encourage you to experiment by adjusting the strip width or using a variety of different widths in each block.

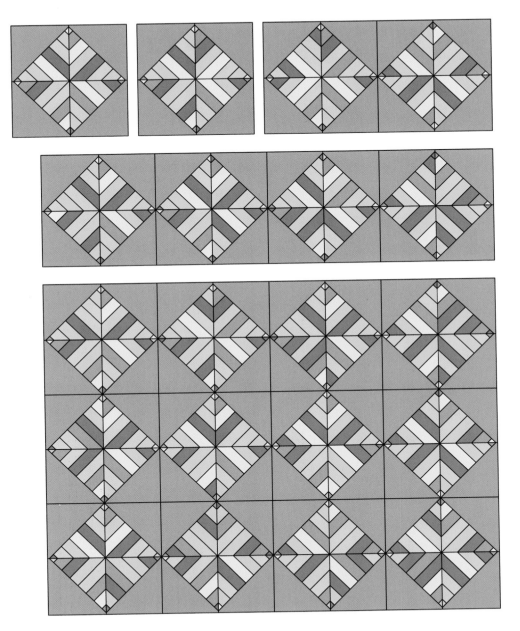

Figure 10

TRIPLICATE

The concept for Triplicate came about out of necessity. I needed to design a quilt that used a minimal amount of fabric, was quick to make, and had a lot of impact. Not asking for much, right? Thanks to a little bit of patchwork and our trusty HST, I came up with something that fitted the bill. This quilt has a lot of movement in the design, in part because of the large amount of negative space. This space is a great opportunity to use a complex quilting design, or to use a contrasting thread to make a simple design pop.

The techniques used in this quilt, and the idea of creating an HST out of an unfinished block, led to the Citrus Peel design (see page 69) and numerous other projects. It is a simple concept but can be executed in many different ways with vastly different results. It is a good lesson in thinking creatively and experimenting with an idea to discover its true potential. I know that there is still more to unearth and make.

FABRIC SELECTION TREATMENT Triplicate uses a triadic color scheme of red orange, mustard yellow, and indigo blue. They are slightly different shades than the primary red, yellow, and blue. I focused on just two prints of each color to keep things simple. The linen background gives the eye a place to rest and tones down the color. Have only a few scraps of your favorite fabrics? This quilt is a great way to showcase them.

Finished HST Size: 10"

Finished Quilt Size: 60" x 80"

Note: Use a ¼" seam allowance throughout.

MATERIALS

Block fabrics: ¼ yard each
of 6 fabrics

Background fabric: 3 yards

Backing fabric: 5 yards

Binding fabric: ⅝ yard

Batting: 68" x 88"

Cutting

From each block fabric, cut:
(2) 4" x WOF strip, subcut strips into
(18) 4" squares

From background fabric, cut:
(6) 10½" x WOF strips, subcut strips
into (24) 10½" squares

(4) 11" x WOF strips, subcut strips
into (12) 11" squares

From binding fabric, cut:
(8) 2½" x WOF strips

Assemble 9-Patch Blocks

1. Sew 4" block squares into (12)
9-patch blocks **(Fig. 1)**. Press the
seams in one direction, alternating
direction every other row. Press the
remaining seam open.

Assemble HSTs

1. Construct 24 HSTs using the
two-at-a-time method (see page 15),
pairing a 9-patch block with an
11" background fabric square
(Fig. 2). Press seams toward the
background fabric. Trim HSTs to
10½" square **(Fig. 3)**.

Assemble Quilt Top

1. Referring to Figure 4, arrange
the HSTs and 10½" background
squares randomly into 8 rows of
6 blocks each. Sew blocks together
in each row. Press seams in one
direction, alternating direction
every other row.

2. Sew rows together. Press the
seams open.

Finishing

1. Cut backing yardage in half. Press.
Trim off the selvages and sew pieces
together lengthwise. Press the
seam open.

2. Baste and quilt as desired.
Bind using your preferred method.

QUILTING TREATMENT

Triplicate was quilted by longarm
quilter Melissa Kelley. I wanted to
play up the HSTs in this quilt, so I
chose an open triangle swirl pattern
for the quilting.

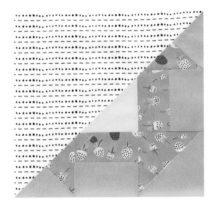

VARIATION

For a twist on this design, replace
the 9-patch blocks with 4-patch,
16-patch, or even a few orphaned
blocks from another project.

Figure 1

Figure 2

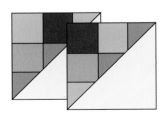

Figure 3

Figure 4

PRISM

The quarter-square triangle (QST) is the cool cousin of the HST. While an HST is a square split into two halves, a QST is a square split into four quadrants. One of the most interesting things about QSTs is how much they change, based on what fabrics are used. Quarter-square triangles made with a print and a solid instantly become the iconic hourglass block. Make them with two prints and they start to resemble some kind of triangular checkerboard. In Prism, the QSTs are composed of four different prints for a completely scrappy look.

There are a few different ways to create QSTs, but this is my favorite way. It is straightforward and yields beautiful, accurate blocks. I like QSTs because they are one of those blocks that look fancy and complicated, but are simple to make. The secret to getting that perfect center seam intersection is to use a consistent seam allowance and to trim accurately as you work.

FABRIC SELECTION TREATMENT I didn't hold back much when choosing fabrics and colors for this quilt. The main colors are fuchsia, coral, mustard, lime green, teal, dark purple, and gray. This quilt, which has a lot of my favorite colors in it, has what I like to call a "controlled scrappy" look. There is a lot going on color-wise, but it is not a complete free-for-all.

Finished HST Size: 7½"

Finished QST Size: 7"

Finished Quilt Size: 70" x 84"

Note: Use a ¼" seam allowance throughout.

MATERIALS

Block fabrics: ¼ yard each of 30 fabrics

Backing fabric: 5¼ yards

Binding fabric: ⅝ yard

Batting: 78" x 92"

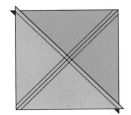

Figure 1

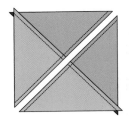

Figure 2

Figure 3

TIP Create any size QST:

Cut Square Size = Finished QST Size + 1½"

Trim QST Size* = Finished QST Size + ½"

*When using a ¼" seam allowance.

Cutting

From each block fabric, cut:
(1) 8½" x WOF strip, subcut strip into (4) 8½" squares

From binding fabric, cut:
(9) 2½" x WOF strips

Assemble HSTs and QSTs

1. Construct 120 HSTs using the two-at-a-time method (see page 15), using two different squares. Press seams to one side. Do not trim.

2. Place 2 untrimmed HSTs right sides together, nestle the seams, and pin in place. Draw a diagonal line across the top HST, perpendicular to the previous seam line. Sew ¼" on either side of that line (**Fig. 1**). Cut

apart and press seam open (**Fig. 2**). Repeat with remaining HSTs to create a total of 120 QSTs. Trim QST blocks to 7½" square (**Fig. 3**).

TIP To ensure that the block is centered when trimming, align the center seam intersection with the 3¾" dot along the 45-degree line on your acrylic ruler.

Assemble Quilt Top

1. Referring to Figure 4, arrange blocks into 12 rows of 10 blocks each. Press seams in one direction, alternating direction every other row.

2. Sew rows together. Press the seams open.

Finishing

1. Cut backing yardage in half. Press. Trim off the selvages and sew pieces together lengthwise. Press the seam open.

2. Baste and quilt as desired. Bind using your preferred method.

QUILTING TREATMENT

For Prism, I used one of my favorite quilting designs: the doodle loop meander. It combines my tried-and-true doodle loops with a traditional meander. This quilting produces an excellent wrinkled texture post-wash, and quilts up quickly.

VARIATION

This quilt is all about color and fabric play. Empty out your scrap bin for a true scrappy look, or focus on a few colors for something a bit more toned down. A monochromatic scheme creates the illusion of transparency and overlap, while still maintaining the classic QST look.

Figure 4

CHAPTER 4

Block Party

Making HSTs is the quilting version of comfort food for me. They are familiar, predictable and filled with massive potential. In this chapter I'll show you 60 (yes 60!) different blocks you can create from 16 simple HST units, arranged into an easy-to-piece four-by-four layout. The three quilts in this section offer a springboard for you to repeat a single block, combine a couple or to create a unique modern sampler quilt. This chapter is all about customization. Use the tools you have gained from the other chapters to play with scale, contrast, color and piecing to design your own perfect HST quilts.

HSTs are such a classic block; to me they are as much a rite of passage in quilting as making a double wedding ring quilt or sewing a log cabin block. HSTs are a building block, and there are so many different ways to use them. One of my favorite ways to use HSTs is in the form of four-by-four quilt blocks. These are easy to make in the traditional 8", 10", and 12" block sizes, and many more. In this chapter, you'll find 60 block mock-ups that can be used to create your own custom quilts or alter designs in this book. I hope this resource will inspire you to experiment and discover your inner quilt designer.

HOW TO USE THE BLOCK CHART

Each block is made up of 16 HSTs, arranged in a four-by-four layout. Creating a custom-sized block is simple: First choose a finished size for your block. Take the finished block size and divide by four; this is the finished size of the HSTs. For example, if I want a 10" finished block, the finished HSTs would be 2½". Choose your preferred HST method (see pages 15–17), and use the provided chart or math to determine the size squares to cut.

The blocks in the chart have four colors each, but the possibilities for each block multiply when the number of colors is adjusted. Use a single color, or as many as 16 to completely change the look of the block. Multiple background fabrics in a single block add even more color and interest. Do not be afraid to experiment.

 TIP Create even more block options by mixing and matching block quarters or halves.

60 Block Chart

CONVERGENCE

This project was the ultimate test for me. I have a relatively short attention span, and I love working on different kinds of projects at the same time. So working on one quilt at a time while making the quilts for this book was challenging. In the interest of efficiency it was best to work this way, but it wasn't without its ups and downs. While I encourage and hope that you will make this quilt, I do recommend breaking it down block by block and giving yourself ample time to make it. With nearly 600 HSTs, this quilt is not for the faint of heart! With all that said, it is so worth the effort, and I am anxious to make another in a different color scheme.

Finished HST Size: 3¹⁄₂"

Finished Block Size: 28"

Finished Quilt Size: 84" x 84"

Note: Use a ¹⁄₄" seam allowance throughout.

FABRIC SELECTION TREATMENT I wanted to keep the colors for Convergence simple and bold, to show off the design, so I chose a gray monochromatic color scheme with the addition of white and an accent color. This formula is pretty foolproof, and a great place to start when choosing the color scheme for this quilt. I used a single print for the background and a variety of prints for each color. This includes an array of white-on-white prints, which do not show well in photographs but is a fun detail in person.

MATERIALS

Fabric A: 1 yard

Fabric B: 2⅝ yards

Fabric C: 1¼ yards

Background fabric: 4½ yards

Backing fabric: 7¾ yards

Binding fabric: ⅝ yard

Batting: 92" x 92"

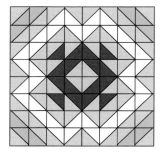

Figure 1

Cutting

From Fabric A, cut:
(5) 6½" x WOF strips, subcut strips into (27) 6½" squares

From Fabric B, cut:
(14) 6½" x WOF strips, subcut strips into (81) 6½" squares

From Fabric C, cut:
(6) 6½" x WOF strips, subcut strips into (36) 6½" squares

From background fabric, cut:
(24) 6½" x WOF strips, subcut strips into (144) 6½" squares

From binding fabric, cut:
(9) 2½" x WOF strips

///// **TIP** Make this quilt even more
///// colorful by creating 9 unique blocks. Each block uses a total of 64 HSTs. Cut 3 squares from Fabric A (¼ yard), 9 from Fabric B (½ yard), 4 from Fabric C (¼ yard), and 16 from the background fabric (⅝ yard).

Assemble HSTs and Blocks

1. Construct 576 HSTs using the four-at-a-time method (see page 16), pairing Fabric A, B, and C squares with background fabric squares. Press seams toward the background fabric. Trim HSTs to 4" square.

2. Each block is made up of 12 Fabric A HSTs, 36 Fabric B HSTs, and 16 Fabric C HSTs. Arrange HSTs in 8 rows of 8 HSTs each **(Fig. 1)**. Sew HSTs together in each row. Press seams in one direction, alternating direction every other row.

3. Sew rows together. Press the seams open.

Assemble Quilt Top

1. Referring to Figure 2, arrange the blocks into 3 rows of 3 blocks each. Press seams in one direction, alternating direction every other row.

2. Sew rows together. Press the seams open.

Finishing

1. Cut backing yardage into thirds. Press. Trim off the selvages and sew pieces together lengthwise. Press the seams open.

2. Baste and quilt as desired. Bind using your preferred method.

QUILTING TREATMENT
I knew from the start I wanted to quilt Convergence with straight lines. I started by quilting two lines diagonally across the entire quilt to form an 'X'. From there, each quadrant was quilted echoing the lines of the 'X'. The quilting lines converge toward the center of the quilt.

VARIATION
Convergence is created with block quarters from three different quilt blocks, all of which can be found in the Block Chart (see page 85). It was fun to play with different combinations before settling on this particular design. Experiment with the placement of these three quarters or use three new ones for a brand-new design. The possibilities are endless!

Figure 2

GETAWAY

One of my favorite things about the projects in this book is that there is no sashing or traditional borders. I have used both many times, and there are times when they are perfectly appropriate and important for a design. However, there is something very satisfying about simply sewing the blocks together and being finished. In the case of Getaway, the absence of sashing transforms the design and the individual block lines disappear.

I think this quilt saw the most changes of any quilt I have made. I decided on a block design pretty quickly, and that never changed, but I spent many months changing the colors and color placement. The beauty of this quilt is that each design has possibilities — the difficult part is choosing which version to make. On the eve of a beach vacation, the final design was based on the desire to travel, relax, and simply get away.

FABRIC SELECTION TREATMENT While I hail from Ohio and live in Wisconsin, I cannot help but daydream about being near the ocean. The color scheme for this quilt was inspired by the sun, sea, and sand. It is light and cheerful, with a fun fuchsia binding as the icing on the cake. The prints are all relatively similar in scale and value, and are primarily monochromatic.

Finished HST Size: 3"

Finished Block Size: 12"

Finished Quilt Size: 48" x 60"

Note: Use a ¼" seam allowance throughout.

MATERIALS

Fabric A: 1 yard

Fabric B: 1 yard

Background fabric: 2 yards

Backing fabric: 3¼ yards

Binding fabric: ½ yard

Batting: 56" x 68"

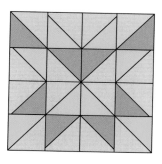

Figure 1

Cutting

From Fabric A, cut:
(4) 8" x WOF strips, subcut strips into (20) 8" squares

From Fabric B, cut:
(4) 8" x WOF strips, subcut strips into (20) 8" squares

From background fabric, cut:
(8) 8" x WOF strips, subcut strips into (40) 8" squares

From binding fabric, cut:
(6) 2½" x WOF strips

Assemble HSTs and Blocks

1. Construct 320 HSTs using the eight-at-a-time method (see page 17), pairing Fabric A and B squares with background fabric squares. Press seams toward background fabric. Trim HSTs to 3½" square **(Fig. 1)**.

2. Each block is made up of 8 Fabric A HSTs and 8 Fabric B HSTs. Refer-ring to Figure 1, arrange HSTs in 4 rows of 4 blocks each. Sew blocks together in each row. Press seams in one direction, alternating direction every other row.

3. Sew rows together. Press the seams open.

Assemble Quilt Top

1. Referring to Figure 2, arrange blocks into 5 rows of 4 blocks each. Press seams in one direction, alternating direction every other row.

TIP If possible, find a place to lay all your blocks out at once. Audition different block orientations, taking a photo of each one. This can make it easier to visualize the finished quilt and acts as a guide while piecing.

2. Sew rows together. Press the seams open.

Finishing

1. Cut backing yardage in half. Press. Trim off the selvages and sew pieces together lengthwise. Press the seam open.

2. Baste and quilt as desired. Bind using your preferred method.

QUILTING TREATMENT

Getaway was another opportunity to play with free-motion swirls. I used a variety of sizes and types of swirls to quilt it, which ended up being good practice. Swirls rely on a bit of muscle memory, so practice really helps make them more consistent and even.

VARIATION

Change up the color placement within the single block design to create a multitude of new patterns. Or, swap out this block with another from the Block Chart (see page 85), and see how the colors play with one another.

Figure 2

PERSPECTIVE

I am a nostalgic and sentimental person. I collect and save many things based on the memories that they spark. This has developed into a love of storytelling. Telling the story behind each quilt that I make is something I practice through writing my blog, as well as through speaking engagements and conversations with friends. Remembering the time in my life when I made a quilt, or the events that led to it, becomes a part of that quilt's story.

I think sampler quilts in particular offer a great opportunity for a story. They are usually long-term projects, which are perfect for making in a group or along with a friend. So grab a friend and make this quilt. The resulting quilt boasts 32 unique blocks and the chance to tell a great story.

Finished HST Size: 3"

Finished Block Size: 12"

Finished Quilt Size: 72" x 96"

Note: Use a ¼" seam allowance throughout.

FABRIC SELECTION TREATMENT Since sampler quilts tend to give me warm fuzzy feelings, I decided to use a color palette of warm colors for Perspective. I used a variety of prints in light, medium, and dark pink, orange, yellow, and gold. In terms of print, I chose a range of large- and small-scale prints, and a good balance of blenders and focus prints. I sprinkled many of my own fabric designs into this quilt, which adds another chapter to its story.

MATERIALS

Block fabrics: ¼ yard each of 16 fabrics

Background fabric: 3 yards

Setting fabric(s): 1 fat quarter each of 16 fabrics

Backing fabric: 6 yards

Binding fabric: ⅝ yard

Batting: 80" x 104"

///// **TIP** If you'd rather use a single print or solid for the Setting fabric, you'll need 2¼ yards. Cut (6) 12½" x WOF strips, subcut strips into (16) 12½" squares.

Cutting

From each block fabric, cut:
(1) 8" x WOF strip, subcut strip into (4) 8" squares

From background fabric, cut:
(13) 8" x WOF strips, subcut strips into (64) 8" squares

From each setting fabric, cut:
(1) 12½" square, for a total of 16 squares

From binding fabric, cut:
(9) 2½" x WOF strips

Assemble HSTs and Blocks

1. Construct 512 HSTs using the eight-at-a-time method (see page 17), pairing block fabric squares with background fabric squares. Press seams toward the block fabric. Trim HSTs to 3½" square.

2. Each block is made up of 16 HSTs. Construct 32 blocks selecting some of your favorite arrangements from the Block Chart (see page 85) and using the 3½" HSTs from Step 1. For each block, sew HSTs together in rows. Press seams in one direction, alternating direction every other row. Sew rows together. Press the seams open.

Assemble Quilt Top

1. Referring to Figure 1, arrange HST blocks and 12½" setting fabric squares into 8 rows of 6 blocks each. Press seams in one direction, alternating direction every other row.

2. Sew rows together. Press the seams open.

Finishing

1. Cut backing yardage in half. Press. Trim off the selvages and sew pieces together lengthwise. Press the seam open.

2. Baste and quilt as desired. Bind using your preferred method.

QUILTING TREATMENT
Perspective was quilted by longarm quilter Melissa Kelley. I love a good swirl, so I chose a simple swirl design for the quilting. With so many different fabrics and block designs, an allover pattern helps mellow it out a little. It would be really interesting for each setting square to have its own quilting design too.

VARIATION
To create your own custom sampler quilt, use your own designs or vary the number of pieced blocks. Fill in the gaps with large squares of your favorite prints, or tone things down with a single solid.

Figure 1

Quilt Coloring Book

Feeling inspired? Grab your colored pencils and use the pages in this coloring book section to experiment with a variety of combinations. Then go back to the project pages and follow the cutting and piecing instructions to make your own quilt.

You will be surprised to see just how easy it is to make each and every one of my designs, yours.

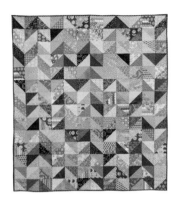

Opposites Attract
p. 35

Interlocked
p. 39

Radiant
p. 43

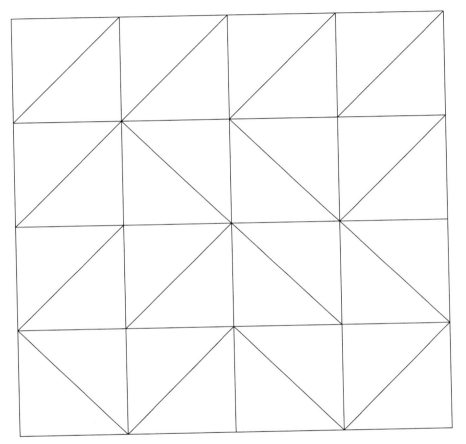

Vast
p. 51

Waypoint
p. 55

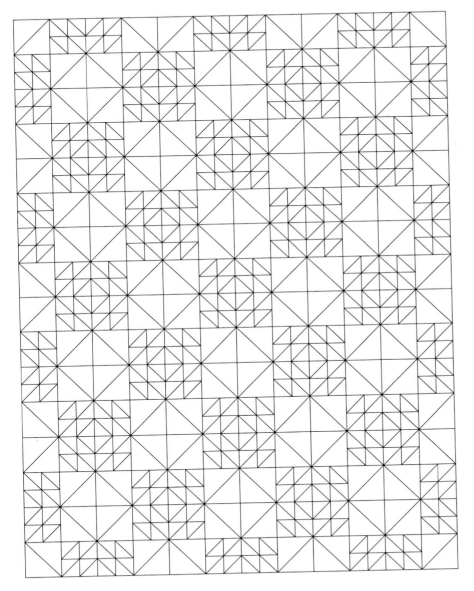

Woven
p. 61

Citrus Peel
p. 69

Triplicate
p. 75

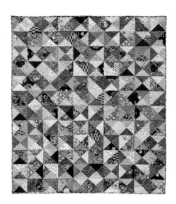

Prism
p. 79

Convergence
p. 101

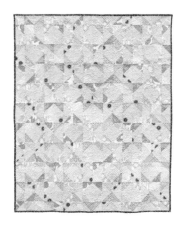

Getaway
p. 105

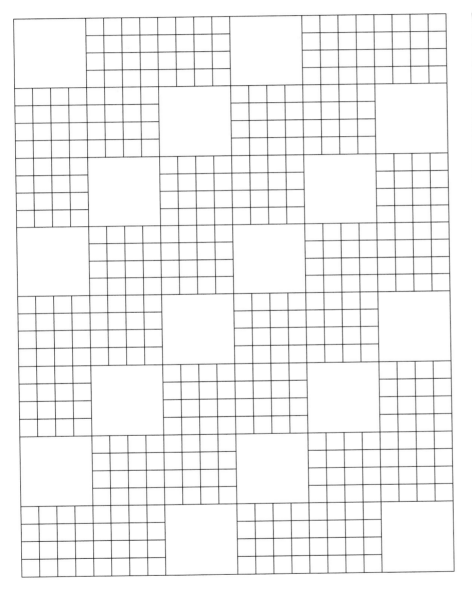

Perspective
p. 109

Supplies and Resources

HST TOOLS

Here are a few of my favorite quilting notions and tools, especially for sewing HSTs:

Art Gallery Fabrics Pure Element Solids
artgalleryfabrics.com
Super-soft and saturated solid fabrics.

Aurifil 50wt Cotton Thread
aurifil.com
My go-to thread for piecing and quilting.

Clover Wonder Clips
clover-usa.com
Great for a variety of applications, but especially for binding.

Janome Sewing Machines
janome.com
Machines for all levels of quilter.

Olfa Rotary Cutters and Mats
olfa.com
The 45mm Quick-Change Rotary Cutter is my favorite cutter.

Omnigrid Rulers
prym-consumer-usa.com/brands/omnigrid
Square rulers are a must-have for trimming HSTs.

Paula Jean Creations Kwik Klip
paulajeancreations.com/kwik-klip.html
Tool for opening and closing basting pins.

Pilot Frixion Pens
pilotpen.us/brands/frixion
Pens erasable by heat.

Quilt in a Day Triangle Square Up Rulers
quiltinaday.com/shoponline/rulers
Trim HSTs in two cuts before pressing.

The Quilting Gypsy Cutting Gizmo
thequiltinggypsy.com
Cut chains quickly and easily with this nifty tool.

Soak Wash Flatter Spray
soakwash.com
A great alternative to spray starch.

The Warm Company Warm and White Batting
warmcompany.com
Low-loft 100% cotton quilt batting.

FABRICS AND NOTIONS

The fabric prints found in this book are from a variety of fabric collections by different manufacturers. Here are a few of my favorite online shops:

Fat Quarter Shop
fatquartershop.com

Hawthorne Threads
hawthornethreads.com

The Intrepid Thread
intrepidthread.com

Pink Castle Fabrics
pinkcastlefabrics.com

The Sewcial Lounge
thesewciallounge.com

About the Author

JENI BAKER has been
sewing since she was 11 years
old, and loves nothing more
than to be surrounded by
fabric. Currently living in
Wisconsin with her pet bunny,
George, Jeni is a licensed
fabric designer for Art Gallery
Fabrics. With a keen eye for
mid-century modern design,
she self-publishes sewing
and quilting patterns for the
modern sewer. Jeni regularly
shares projects and tutorials
on her blog, *In Color Order*
(incolororder.com). She is
always looking for ways to be
creative every day, and simply
enjoys living a handmade
life. In addition to sewing,
her hobbies include knitting,
photography, baking, and
collecting vintage
kitchenware and linens.